Original title:
Starry Veil

Copyright © 2024 Swan Charm
All rights reserved.

Author: Sebastian Sarapuu
ISBN HARDBACK: 978-9916-79-444-9
ISBN PAPERBACK: 978-9916-79-445-6
ISBN EBOOK: 978-9916-79-446-3

Dreams that Paint the Twilight

In twilight's glow, dreams softly hum,
Whispers of night, a gentle strum.
Colors blend, as shadows play,
Hopes take flight, at the end of day.

Stars begin to wink and shine,
Casting light on a path divine.
Each dream a brush, each thought a hue,
Painting skies of deepest blue.

A canvas stretches, wide and bright,
With whispers of love that ignite.
Memories dance on the evening breeze,
Encouraging hearts to feel at ease.

With every sigh, a story spins,
Evening sighs held on the winds.
Fleeting moments, captured so sweet,
In dreams that make the night complete.

As shadows stretch and daylight fades,
New dreams emerge, and hope cascades.
In the twilight, we'll find our way,
Crafted by dreams, till break of day.

The Silent Watchers

In shadows deep, they wait and sigh,
With eyes like stars, they softly pry.
The world below, it hums and breathes,
Yet in their gaze, time seldom leaves.

Ancient trees, their whispered tales,
Of fleeting dreams and gentle gales.
They guard the night, the fleeting light,
In silence fierce, they hold the night.

Ethereal Quilts of Night

Stars scatter like threads of gold,
In a quilt of night, mysteries hold.
Each twinkle whispers secrets deep,
While all the world in slumber sleeps.

The moon weaves silver through the skies,
A tapestry where shadows rise.
Beneath this cover, dreams take flight,
In ethereal quilts, the heart ignites.

A Galaxy of Murmurs

Waves of whispers, soft and low,
A cosmic dance, a silent flow.
Between the stars, a language feels,
In every breath, the universe reveals.

Hushed tones echo, sweetly glide,
Through nebulas, where secrets hide.
In every twinkling orb arrives,
An echo of where wonder thrives.

Glimmers in the Gloom

In twilight hours, the world turns grey,
Yet tiny sparks still find their way.
A flicker bright, in darkest night,
Reminds the heart of hope and light.

Beneath the clouds, the starlit dance,
A chance to dream, a fleeting chance.
With glimmers bold, they pierce the shroud,
In silence wrapped, they stand aloud.

In the Quiet of Star-Mists

In the quiet of star-mists,
Whispers dance on the breeze,
Dreams take flight on soft sighs,
Embraced by night's gentle ease.

Silver tears of the heavens,
Glisten on the dark sea,
Each twinkle a soft promise,
Of what is yet to be.

Echoes of laughter linger,
Lost in time's tender fold,
The secrets of the cosmos,
In silence, they unfold.

A world wrapped in shadows,
Where the wild spirits roam,
In the quiet of star-mists,
We find our way back home.

Beneath the watchful moonlight,
Hearts weave tales of old,
In the quiet of memories,
New stories are retold.

Where Time Stretches Thin

In the twilight's sweet embrace,
Where time stretches thin and soft,
Moments linger like soft sighs,
In a world that feels aloft.

Gentle hands of the past,
Caress the fragile now,
Each second a fleeting spark,
In another's furrowed brow.

Whispers of long-lost echoes,
Chase shadows on the wall,
In this space between heartbeats,
We feel the rise and fall.

The hours stretch like twilight,
Softly bending, then they break,
In the stillness of the present,
Time reminds us, for our sake.

Here is where dreams awaken,
In the hush before the dawn,
Where time stretches like ribbons,
In a tapestry outdrawn.

Reflections in the Midnight Hour

In reflections of the midnight hour,
Whispers haunt the darkened space,
Shadows dance, a spectral power,
Caught in time's unending chase.

The moon, a silver sentinel,
Watches o'er the velvet night,
Casting dreams like fragile shells,
Glistening in borrowed light.

Each heartbeat, a quiet echo,
Ripples through the still expanse,
In this realm where time's but shadow,
Fate beckons us to dance.

Lost in thought, the world retreats,
Where silence wraps its gentle shroud,
In the midnight hour, heartbeats,
Speak truths that are not loud.

Here we find our hidden selves,
In the depths of night's embrace,
Reflections in the midnight hour,
Reveal our truest face.

Fragments of Eternal Glow

In fragments of eternal glow,
We find pieces of our souls,
Scattered dust on the winds of time,
With stories yet untold.

Moments flicker like candles,
Filling the air with their light,
Each whisper a soft reminder,
That darkness follows bright.

In the dance of shadows' play,
We seek warmth in fleeting beams,
In fragments of a timeless past,
Lie the remnants of our dreams.

Threads of gold intertwine,
In the tapestry of night,
Each fragment a part of something,
Beautiful in its fight.

As stars bleed into morning,
And daylight begins to sew,
We collect the shining pieces,
From fragments of eternal glow.

Secrets of the Galactic Bloom

In whispers soft the stars align,
Their colors weave a tale divine.
Petals stretch in cosmic grace,
Each bloom a dream, a silent space.

Galaxies swirl in velvet air,
With every twist, a secret rare.
The night unveils its hidden lore,
As echoes dance forevermore.

Stardust clings to ancient stones,
Reflecting on the heart's deep tones.
A tapestry of light unfolds,
Where every story quietly holds.

In shadows cast by moonlight's beam,
The universe ignites a dream.
Each heartbeat sings a vibrant note,
Through cosmic gardens, whispers float.

Eternity breaths through time's embrace,
While luminous wonders find their place.
In the galactic bloom's soft sigh,
A truth unwinds, as stars draw nigh.

Horizons of Enchantment

Where twilight paints the skies with gold,
The heart is open, stories told.
Waves of wonder touch the shore,
In every sigh, enchantment's core.

Mountains whisper in the breeze,
Secrets nestled in the trees.
Each leaf dances with tales untold,
Horizons shift as dreams unfold.

The sun dips low in amber light,
A magical and fleeting sight.
Beneath the stars, the world awakes,
In quietude, the heart remakes.

Bridges span from night to day,
In every shade, the soul can play.
With open arms, the horizon calls,
A lover's touch where spirit falls.

In twilight's arms, we'll roam and find,
The spark of life, both brave and kind.
Horizons wide, our dreams ascend,
An endless journey, without end.

Mysteries in the Cosmic Night

The moonlight whispers secrets old,
Of galaxies in stories bold.
Each twinkle holds a dreamer's wish,
In vast expanse, a cosmic dish.

Nebulas weave in colors bright,
Painting canvases of the night.
Constellations draw their threads,
In silent tales, the cosmos spreads.

Each falling star, a fleeting glance,
A moment grasped in endless dance.
The universe breathes, and time stands still,
As dark meets light, a quest fulfilled.

Layers deep within the void,
Unearthed truths cannot be toyed.
In shadows rich, the dreams ignite,
A symphony of cosmic light.

Within this night, the heart beats strong,
Entwined with stars, where we belong.
Mysteries call from depths untamed,
In the cosmic night, we are named.

Hues of Dusk and Dawn

When dusk descends, the colors gleam,
A palette drawn from twilight's dream.
Fading light, a soft embrace,
Where night shall weave its whispered grace.

The morn awakens with tender light,
Transforming shadows into sight.
Colors burst as daylight breaks,
In every hue, a chance awakes.

From purples deep to golds that shine,
The sky becomes a canvas fine.
Each moment painted, fleeting bliss,
In hues that dance, we find our kiss.

With every breath, the colors blend,
A cycle spun, from start to end.
Dusk and dawn entwined in play,
Remind us of the fleeting day.

In this embrace, the world will spin,
In every loss, we find the win.
The hues of life, they intertwine,
A masterpiece, forever shine.

Threads of Enchantment

In the twilight, whispers weave,
Magic lingers, dreams believe.
Colors dance in soft embrace,
Time stands still, a sacred space.

Gentle murmurs, secrets share,
In the air, a timeless prayer.
Every stitch a tale untold,
Woven deep, in hearts of gold.

Through the forest, shadows play,
Guiding travelers on their way.
Stars above become the guide,
In this realm, we must confide.

Threaded paths through night and day,
Leading souls who wish to stay.
In the silence, magic grows,
Life's sweet rhythm softly flows.

Embraced by night's velvet shroud,
In this moment, hearts are loud.
Together we can weave and spin,
A tapestry where dreams begin.

Cosmic Constellations

In the night, stars align bright,
Whispers of the dark invite.
Each dot a story, time unfurls,
Mapping dreams in silver swirls.

Galaxies in silent dance,
Twinkling eyes, a fleeting glance.
Gravity binds the lost and found,
In the void, enchantments abound.

The moon's glow, a guiding light,
Painting shadows in the night.
Hope ignites in vast expanse,
Cosmic journeys start by chance.

Planets spin in rhythmic grace,
Infinite, an open space.
Through the silence, starlight beams,
We are stardust, born from dreams.

In this dance of endless skies,
Whispers echo, soft goodbyes.
Each moment, a glimpse divine,
In the cosmos, pure design.

Moonlit Fantasia

Beneath the moon's enchanting glow,
Fantasy begins to flow.
Dancing shadows, silver light,
Painting dreams of pure delight.

Waves of whispers fill the air,
Magic hangs, a soft affair.
In this world where dreams ignite,
Every heart can take flight.

Petals fall in gentle breeze,
Nature sighs with graceful ease.
Lost in thoughts, a tranquil night,
Hopeful souls embrace the light.

With each shimmer, tales unfold,
Nighttime secrets, softly told.
Through the stars, we journey far,
Guided by our wish upon a star.

In this realm of dreams and fate,
Every heartbeat resonates.
Moonlit fantasia, a sweet song,
In this magic, we belong.

The Etherial Silence

In the hush of twilight's grace,
Time suspends in sacred space.
Whispers linger on the breeze,
Carrying secrets from the trees.

Softly glows the setting sun,
Day's embrace is almost done.
Moments pause in breathless air,
Infinite, with love to share.

Each heartbeat echoes in the still,
Binding dreams to ancient will.
In this silence, truths reside,
Open hearts we cannot hide.

Stars awaken, softly gleam,
Illuminating every dream.
With each pulse, we drift and sway,
In the night, we find our way.

The etherial silence calls,
Through the heavens, inspiration falls.
In this quiet, we are one,
A symphony that's just begun.

The Night's Embrace

In shadows deep, the world does sleep,
The moonlight weaves a dream to keep.
Silence whispers soft and low,
While stars above begin to glow.

Gentle breezes dance and twirl,
In this serene and starlit swirl.
Each heartbeat flutters, sweet and pure,
Wrapped in night, a heart feels sure.

The clock ticks softly, time stands still,
As magic drapes each quiet hill.
The night's embrace, a soft caress,
Brings peace and calm, deep happiness.

Crickets chirp their lullaby,
Underneath the vast black sky.
Dreams take flight on whispered wings,
While night reveals what solace brings.

In starlit paths, our hopes align,
With every breath, the stars define.
In night's embrace, we find our way,
To brighter dawns, to each new day.

Astral Serenade

A melody drifts through the night,
Stars dance to a tune, pure and bright.
Galaxies spin in graceful arcs,
While silence listens for cosmic sparks.

Notes of twilight softly fall,
Like whispers among the shadows tall.
Constellations hum their ancient song,
As time flows gently, wild yet strong.

The universe sways in graceful tune,
Beneath the watchful, silver moon.
Celestial rhythms beat the air,
In every corner, beauty rare.

Planets shimmer in the vast expanse,
Inviting all to join the dance.
Through cosmic wonders, we are swayed,
In harmony, our hearts arrayed.

An astral lullaby softly plays,
Carried on the night's soft gaze.
With every heartbeat, we find grace,
In this serene and starry place.

Radiant Pinpricks of Wonder

On velvet skies, the stars ignite,
Pinpricks shining through the night.
A canvas vast, both deep and wide,
Where dreams and wishes dare abide.

Each spark a tale, a whispered thought,
Of hopes achieved, of battles fought.
In radiant glow, they whisper clear,
That in the dark, we conquer fear.

A galaxy of stories waits,
To share its wonders, open gates.
The night unveils, with glimmering light,
A world alive, with pure delight.

With every twinkle, hearts anew,
In cosmic beauty, we find our view.
These pinpricks shine, a guiding flame,
Reminding us we're all the same.

In silence deep, beneath the stars,
We find our strength, no matter scars.
Radiant hope in night we see,
In every pinprick, we are free.

Nocturnal Canvas

The night unfurls its darkened sheet,
A canvas rich where shadows meet.
Brushstrokes of stars, a sight to see,
An art of dreams, wild and free.

Vivid colors in moonlit beams,
Painted stories woven from dreams.
The brush of night creates a scene,
Where every star becomes a queen.

Echoes of wonder fill the air,
As creatures of dusk shake off their care.
A masterpiece of peace unfolds,
In hues of silence, magic holds.

With every sigh, the world transforms,
In this nocturnal realm, life warms.
A tranquil heart, a gentle space,
The night's embrace, a soft embrace.

Under the stars, our spirits soar,
Each moment cherished, so much more.
In this dark canvas, we find grace,
As night paints love on time and space.

A Melodic Nightscape

In the hush of twilight's embrace,
Stars whisper secrets, soft and clear,
Moonlight dances, a gentle grace,
Creating dreams that linger near.

Shadows weave through the silver trees,
Echoes of laughter fill the air,
Nature sings with a tranquil ease,
Melodies blending everywhere.

Waves of longing on the breeze,
Crescendo of hearts in sweet refrain,
Every sound a comforting tease,
Memories forming like gentle rain.

Time stands still in this serenade,
Bathed in hues of deep indigo,
Beyond the veil where dreams are made,
A night where only spirits flow.

As dawn approaches, the music fades,
Yet in the heart, the echoes stay,
A melodic nightscape never jades,
For in our souls, it finds a way.

Timeless Elysium

In fields where golden blossoms sway,
Time retreats, embracing peace,
Whispers of joy in bright display,
A haven where all troubles cease.

Crystal waters mirror the sky,
Reflecting dreams both fierce and bright,
Every moment a gentle sigh,
In endless grace, we find our light.

Beneath the shade of ancient trees,
We wander paths of soft delight,
Nature's symphony on the breeze,
In this realm, the world feels right.

With each step, the hearts do soar,
Carried by the wind's sweet song,
A timeless dance forevermore,
In Elysium, where we belong.

When shadows threaten to draw near,
The light within will guide the way,
In timeless Elysium, we steer,
For love and hope will always stay.

Horizon of Dreams

At dusk where colors softly blend,
The horizon whispers tales untold,
Every sunset brings a friend,
A canvas rich with shades of gold.

Winds of promise stirring the night,
Carried on wings of distant flight,
Every star ignites a spark,
In the sky, we leave our mark.

As the twilight unfolds its grace,
Dreams awaken from their slumber,
In the twilight's warm embrace,
Possibilities begin to ponder.

Crickets serenade the moon,
Nature's orchestra fills the air,
While the world hums a gentle tune,
We embark on journeys rare.

In the stillness, hope takes flight,
Toward a horizon vast and wide,
In a realm of endless light,
Where all our dreams can safely hide.

Ethereal Dusk

As daylight whispers its last goodbye,
The sky dons robes of lavender hues,
Stars ignite and begin to sigh,
In the twilight's soft, serene muse.

Veils of mist caress the ground,
Moonbeams glisten on dewy leaves,
In silence, magic can be found,
In the heart, the spirit believes.

Colors fade in graceful dance,
While shadows stretch and softly play,
In this moment, take a chance,
To surrender to night's array.

Whispers of dreams in the air,
Carried by breezes, sweet and light,
In this dusk, we have a prayer,
A wish upon a falling light.

Ethereal dusk, a time so kind,
Where chaos melts like morning dew,
In each heartbeat, we unwind,
Together, we'll chase the view.

The Language of Light

In prisms bright, the colors play,
Each beam a word that lights the way.
A dance of hues in silent flight,
Whispers of joy, the language of light.

Through morning's glow, the world awakes,
A canvas born where sunlight breaks.
In shadows deep, the secrets hide,
Echoes of dreams where hopes abide.

A flicker speaks of love's embrace,
In every ray, a warm caress.
Reflections glint, the heart ignites,
In every spark, the spirit's heights.

Each twilight's kiss, a promise sweet,
In fading light, our souls shall meet.
From dusk to dawn, an endless flight,
We find our truth in the language of light.

Dreaming in Nebulae

In cosmic clouds, our dreams unfold,
Colors swirl like whispers bold.
Galaxies bloom in gentle sway,
We drift in peace, lost in the play.

Stars ignite the velvet night,
Guiding us with silver light.
In every breath, the stardust sings,
The universe, a tapestry of wings.

We float on thoughts of distant shores,
Where time and space open doors.
Imagination's flight takes hold,
In dreams of nebulae, we are enfolded.

Through cosmic tides, our spirits roam,
In silent realms, we find our home.
With every pulse, the cosmos sighs,
As we awaken to the skies.

Skies Woven with Lullabies

Hear the whispers of the night,
Soft as feathers, pure and light.
Moonbeams cradle souls in flight,
Skies woven with lullabies, so bright.

In gentle winds, sweet tunes arise,
Carried on air, beneath the skies.
Stars twinkle like the softest eyes,
Guiding dreams in serenades that rise.

Each note a balm for weary minds,
A symphony of love that binds.
With every breath, the world complies,
As hearts are wrapped in these lullabies.

Through starlit nights, our hopes take wing,
In harmony, our spirits sing.
In twilight's hush, beneath the sighs,
We find our peace, in lullabies.

Beyond the Darkened Spin

In shadows where the lost reside,
We seek the light, the truth inside.
Through twisted paths, we take our flight,
Beyond the darkened spin, we write.

A journey deep through forgotten tales,
Where courage blooms and fear pales.
In every heart, a spark ignites,
Guiding us through the endless nights.

With every turn, the stars align,
Beneath the weight of time, we shine.
In every voice, the echoes blend,
A symphony where dreams transcend.

Through every shadow, we shall tread,
With dreams of light, we forge ahead.
United in our hopes, we win,
As we rise beyond the darkened spin.

Dance of the Midnight Skies

Underneath the moon's soft glow,
Stars begin their gentle show.
Whispers float on night's cool breeze,
As shadows sway among the trees.

A melody of twinkling lights,
Dancing through the starry nights.
Time stands still, the world at ease,
In the symphony that nature frees.

The cosmos twirls in playful glee,
Awakening dreams, setting them free.
In the quiet of this endless space,
We find our place, we find our grace.

With every heartbeat, every sigh,
We rise and fall like waves on high.
Together in the night's embrace,
We lose ourselves, we find our grace.

In this dance of the midnight skies,
Where time is lost, and wonder lies.
The universe sings a secret song,
In this moment, we truly belong.

Shimmering Shadows Above

Across the vast and endless night,
Shadows weave in soft moonlight.
Each twinkle tells a tale untold,
A tapestry of dreams unrolled.

Beneath the stars, they lightly tread,
In silent steps, where journeys led.
Shimmering whispers fill the air,
Of ancient tales and secret care.

A cosmic dance of light and dark,
Each shadow shines, each light sparks.
In unity, they swirl and play,
A ballet of night, a vibrant array.

As dusk embraces the dawn's warm glow,
The shimmering shadows start to flow.
In every heart, they leave a trace,
A moment shared, a sacred space.

Thus, in the night, we find our way,
In shimmering shadows, we choose to stay.
With every breath and every sigh,
Our souls connect beneath the sky.

Veils of Stardust

Veils of stardust drape the night,
Whispers of celestial light.
Each twinkling speck, a moment caught,
In dreams that dance, in hopes sought.

Cosmic raindrops fall like tears,
Carrying with them all our fears.
Yet from these tears, our wishes bloom,
In darkened skies, they carve their room.

Galaxies spin with timeless grace,
In their embrace, we find our place.
Floating gently on light's soft tide,
Where every heartache learns to bide.

In the vastness, we are one,
Under the watch of moon and sun.
Veils of stardust guide our dreams,
In this universe, nothing's as it seems.

So breathe in deep the night's sweet air,
Let stardust showers wash your care.
Within their glow, we dance and play,
As the cosmos swirls and fades away.

A Cosmos of Secrets

In shadows deep, the cosmos sighs,
Carrying whispers from the skies.
Secrets held in each star's light,
Guiding dreamers through the night.

Every twinkle, a story spun,
Of battles lost, and victories won.
The universe, a canvas vast,
Painting futures from the past.

Among the stars, we search and roam,
Finding pieces of our home.
In the silence, echoes call,
Uniting souls, connecting all.

As galaxies shimmer, so do our hearts,
In the dance of life, where wonder starts.
Each secret shared, a lighted spark,
Illuminating paths through the dark.

And when the dawn begins to break,
We'll carry forth what stardust makes.
In every breath, we'll find and see,
The cosmos breathing inside of me.

Nightfall's Latticework

The stars weave tales in the deep night,
A tapestry of silken light.
Each twinkle speaks of dreams untold,
In shadows warm, the night unfolds.

Whispers of winds through the trees bend,
Echoes of secrets that night will send.
Beneath the moon, the world finds rest,
In blanket dark, we feel so blessed.

Crickets chant in their soft refrain,
While distant sirens softly wane.
The velvet dusk wraps time in still,
A gentle pause, the heart to fill.

As twilight drapes her azure cloak,
We drift with thoughts that softly soak.
In this embrace of time divine,
The night's sweet hush becomes our wine.

So let the night be our retreat,
Where dreams and reality gently meet.
In nightfall's care, we find our way,
A woven path till break of day.

Glimmers of Infinite Wonder

In the vast sky, stars begin to play,
Each glitter a promise, bright as day.
Galaxies swirl in a cosmic dance,
Inviting our hearts to dream and glance.

Endless horizons, mysteries vast,
Echoes of futures and whispers of past.
In silence, wisdom like rivers flow,
Through paths of starlight, our minds will go.

Shooting stars streak through the night,
Painting wishes in luminous flight.
With every spark, we can explore,
The boundless dreams forevermore.

Celestial bodies, ancient and wise,
Guide us through dark with shimmering eyes.
In this grand theater of cosmic lore,
We find ourselves wanting to soar.

Glimmers unite, a dance of delight,
Each flicker a chance to ignite.
In infinite wonder we deeply trust,
For in the cosmos, we are all dust.

A Symphony of Distant Worlds

Beyond the void, the stars do sing,
A melody from the cosmos brings.
Notes of planets, far and wide,
In harmony, they swell and glide.

Each world a story, each note a tale,
In rhythmic pulses, we set our sail.
Bright comets trail their liquid light,
While moons sway gently in the night.

Galactic whispers roll through the dark,
Inviting souls to leave their mark.
In this grand symphony of space,
We find our fears and hopes embrace.

From void to vibrant, life's refrain,
Distant echoes, a sweet sustain.
Through cosmic chords, we learn to feel,
The vast connection that is so real.

As we dance through these starry seas,
With every beat, our hearts find ease.
In unity, we play our part,
A symphony of worlds, hand to heart.

Interstellar Whispers

Through the cosmos, whispers float,
Messages on every comet's coat.
Stories wrapped in stardust dreams,
Traveling far on lunar beams.

Each breath of space holds a secret hope,
In celestial currents, we learn to cope.
Signals drifting from realms unknown,
Kindred spirits on journeys flown.

Nebulas bloom with colors bright,
Painting the dark with dazzling light.
In the silence, the heart can hear,
Echoes of stars that draw us near.

As galaxies turn in timeless grace,
We find our place in the vast embrace.
In every twinkle, a thought of you,
Interstellar whispers in every hue.

Together we drift on cosmic tides,
With every pulse, the universe abides.
In this dance of light, forever twinned,
We're lost in whispers; our souls rescind.

The Fabric of the Universe

Stitched with stars and longing dreams,
Woven paths that twist and gleam.
Each thread a tale of cosmic flight,
In darkened skies, our hearts ignite.

Galaxies dance in endless night,
A tapestry of purest light.
Entangled fates and silent sighs,
Dance through the vastness, where hope lies.

Hearts echo back the ancient call,
In stellar realms, we rise and fall.
The threads of time, a sacred weave,
In the embrace of dawn, we believe.

Nebulae cradle our wishes tight,
In the embrace of endless night.
The fabric holds both joy and pain,
Yet in its folds, love shall remain.

From stardust born, to stars we drift,
In every weave, a timeless gift.
Together we bloom in light's own grace,
Threads of the universe we embrace.

Whispers Beneath the Cosmic Veil

In silence deep, the echoes find,
A gentle touch, a breath entwined.
Whispers of light in shadows dance,
Beneath the veil, we glimpse romance.

The moon's soft glow, a guiding hand,
Across the stars, where dreams expand.
In twilight's hush, secrets reside,
Starlit wishes, our hearts confide.

Galactic winds in tender flight,
Carry our hopes through the night.
Beneath the veil, the cosmos sings,
Of ancient truths and fleeting things.

In every twinkle, stories swell,
With cada note, we weave our spell.
Together lost, in astral play,
Beneath the night, we drift away.

The galaxy calls, a siren's plea,
In timeless realms, just you and me.
Under the cosmic veil so bright,
We find forever in the night.

A Canvas of Distant Lights

A canvas stretched across the skies,
With pigments bold, the starlight lies.
Infinity paints with every hue,
In celestial art, we find what's true.

Vibrant swirls of dusk and dawn,
In constellations, we are drawn.
Each flicker tells a tale untold,
Of galaxies vast, and dreams of gold.

Beneath this art, our spirits soar,
Comets streak, and hearts explore.
We dream in colors, bright and rare,
Adrift in wonder, beyond compare.

This cosmic gallery we share,
In every light, a whispered prayer.
So let us dance 'neath twinkling sights,
On this vast canvas of distant lights.

Together we roam through space and time,
In every shadow, a reason sublime.
A masterpiece of love and fate,
Within the stars, we celebrate.

Glittering Emissaries

Glittering emissaries from afar,
Silent travelers, each a star.
They guide us through the velvet dark,
In their glow, we find the spark.

Meteors blaze with fleeting grace,
In their wake, they leave a trace.
Messages carried through the night,
A dance of dreams, a flickering light.

Celestial whispers in cosmic flight,
Igniting paths, igniting sight.
In every shimmer, stories thrive,
Of journeys taken, of dreams alive.

The night unfolds, a tapestry bright,
With emissaries of love's own light.
Silent companions, never stray,
In their embrace, we find our way.

Hold close their glow, let hopes arise,
In the cosmic cradle, we find the skies.
Glittering emissaries, our hearts' decree,
Guide us gently, eternally free.

Symphonic Whispers in Black

In shadows deep, the silence grows,
Soft melodies, as night bestows.
Whispers of dreams in velvet skies,
Echoes of time where the spirit flies.

Notes of the moon, a silver gleam,
Dancing lightly on a breathless stream.
Harmonies weave through the quiet air,
Carrying secrets with tender care.

A canvas vast, painted in night,
Stars like silver, glimmering bright.
In the stillness, a symphony swells,
Each note a story, each silence tells.

Drifting softly on a breeze's sigh,
A lullaby woven from the sky.
Embers of twilight, dusk's soft embrace,
In the dark, we find our place.

A Journey Amongst the Stars

Beneath the arch of twilight's grace,
We set our sights on a distant place.
Galaxies twirl in a cosmic dance,
Inviting hearts for a dreamlike chance.

Through glowing trails and shooting lights,
We navigate the celestial nights.
Every twinkle, a whispered dream,
Guiding us further into the gleam.

Constellations map the paths we take,
Stories hidden in the space awake.
With every breath, the universe sings,
Echoing truths that wonder brings.

In the fabric of stardust's embrace,
We chase the light, we find our place.
Eternity's charm, a radiant hue,
As we drift in dreams, me and you.

Ethereal Explorations

Through misty realms and whispers light,
We wander softly, a curious flight.
In the corners of a fading dream,
Where shadows merge with the silver beam.

Time floats gently, a feathered grace,
In the heart of night, we find our space.
Luminous echoes, an ageless tale,
Calling through valleys where legends sail.

The ether glows with untold lore,
Each whisper inviting us to explore.
In the silence, a world unfolds,
Mysteries wrapped in ancient folds.

With every step, we leave our mark,
Illuminated paths in the dark.
In these explorations, we ignite,
The beauty of dreams in gentle light.

Chasing Luminous Memories

Flickering moments, like fireflies,
Captured in echoes of tender sighs.
Memories dance in the softest glow,
Trailing whispers of all we know.

Each golden hue, a cherished thought,
In the tapestry of love, we're caught.
As time draws breath, we weave anew,
With threads of laughter and skies so blue.

Chasing the light of days gone by,
Through twilight hues and sapphire sky.
Every heartbeat, a rhythm's trace,
In luminous dreams, we find our place.

A journey unfolds in each fleeting turn,
The warmth of memories, forever yearn.
In this sweet chase, we learn to see,
Life's luminous moments, wild and free.

Aurora's Hidden Palette

In the dawn's embrace, colors collide,
Whispers of light in the sky abide.
Every hue tells an ancient tale,
As darkness fades, the wonders unveil.

Brushstrokes of gold and blush appear,
Painting dreams that all hold dear.
Nature's canvas, vast and wide,
Inspiring hearts, where hopes reside.

Beneath the dance of vibrant rays,
Life awakens, in myriad ways.
Soft glimmers spark the tranquil night,
In every shadow, a glimpse of light.

For in the twilight's gentle hold,
Stories of ages, silent yet bold.
Aurora sings, with colors bright,
A symphony woven in day's first light.

The Universe in a Teardrop

A single teardrop, a precious sphere,
Reflects the cosmos, deep and clear.
Stars and galaxies swirl within,
A universe born from joy and sin.

In sorrow's grasp, beauty takes form,
Emotions twist, like a brewing storm.
Every drip, a story untold,
A journey through heart, fearless and bold.

Time flows slow in this fragile glass,
Moments captured, destined to pass.
In silent weeping, wisdom hides,
The strength of love, where hope abides.

Look deeper still into this sea,
Find the answers that set you free.
For within this drop, a world can bloom,
In its depths lies light amidst the gloom.

Songs of the Wandering Stars

Stars wander through the night's grand stage,
Echoing songs from a distant age.
Twinkling softly, their tales unfold,
In whispers of light, legends retold.

Chasing shadows, they dance and sway,
Guiding lost souls along their way.
Each flicker a note in the cosmic tune,
A melody played to the silver moon.

Through the vastness, their voices rise,
Crafting harmonies across the skies.
In the stillness, the universe sighs,
As wandering stars sing lullabies.

Let their brilliance wash over you,
Painting the night in vibrant hues.
For above us all, they sing and roam,
Our celestial kin, forever home.

Celestial Melodies

From bright horizons, songs are spun,
In celestial realms, they are begun.
The moon's soft glow, a serenade,
Sings of dreams in night's cascade.

Comets streak through endless space,
Leaving trails of light, a fiery grace.
Each note a heartbeat, timeless and true,
Binding the cosmos, me and you.

Galaxies collide in a rhythmic dance,
Creating harmonies that entrance.
In this vast choir, hearts unite,
Wrapped in the warmth of starlit night.

Beyond the veil of twilight skies,
The music of worlds in silence lies.
Listen closely, let your spirit soar,
For in these melodies, we are evermore.

The Promise of Tomorrow's Dawn

In the quiet, whispers call,
Hope emerges, standing tall.
Colors of the rising light,
Chase away the cloak of night.

The horizon paints its glow,
Dreams awaken, seeds to sow.
Morning breaks with gentle care,
Promises bloom in the air.

Every ray a tender touch,
Guiding hearts that long for much.
Step by step, we greet the day,
In its warmth, we'll find our way.

Nature sings a vibrant tune,
Nestled in the sun's sweet boon.
Tomorrow's hopes, a canvas wide,
On this journey, we'll abide.

As the stars fade from our sight,
We embrace the new sunlight.
With each dawn, a chance given,
To rise and soar, our spirits riven.

Tides of the Celestial Sea

Waves of silver, soft and bright,
Dance beneath the moon's soft light.
Whispers drift on evening air,
Secrets spun with tender care.

Stars like pearls on velvet spread,
Guiding dreams where hearts are led.
Currents pull in silent grace,
Ebb and flow in time and space.

Cosmic winds begin to weave,
Stories that we long believe.
Ocean depths of starlit lore,
Carrying us to distant shore.

Nights unfurl in shades of blue,
Endless skies, a world anew.
In the depths, our spirits roam,
Finding peace, forever home.

Each tide brings a promise near,
Casting away our old fears.
With every wave, we sail so free,
Boundless love in the celestial sea.

Echoes of Nightfall

As shadows blend with whispered dreams,
Night unfolds in silver themes.
The world hushes, calm descends,
In darkness, hope still transcends.

Stars emerge with quiet grace,
Guiding lost souls through the space.
Each heartbeat resonates bold,
In the night, our tales are told.

Moonlight weaves through ancient trees,
Dancing softly on the breeze.
Echoes of the day's delight,
Live anew in silent night.

As the sky holds secrets tight,
We gather strength, hearts in flight.
With open arms, we greet the dark,
Ready now to find our spark.

In this realm where shadows play,
We become what dreams convey.
Together in the stillness found,
We rise with echoes, earthward bound.

Illuminated Traces of Dreams

In the cradle of the night,
Dreams like lanterns burn so bright.
Guiding souls through velvet skies,
Where hopes whisper and softly rise.

Footsteps trace on silver beams,
Marking all our hidden dreams.
Every thought a fleeting flame,
Illuminating every name.

Through the dark, we weave our path,
Collecting joy, releasing wrath.
With each breath, our spirits soar,
Chasing visions evermore.

The dawn may hide within the night,
But embers glow with pure delight.
In the shadows, futures gleam,
Crafting every fragile dream.

We journey soft on stardust trails,
Guided by the nightingale's wails.
In the tapestry we weave,
Illuminated hopes believe.

Celestial Flare

In the sky, a burning hue,
Stars igniting, bright and new.
Galaxies swirl, a timeless dance,
Moments lost in cosmic trance.

Nebulas glow with colors rare,
Whispers of dreams float in the air.
Planets spin in silent grace,
Eternal tales in vast embrace.

Waves of light, so fiercely spread,
Chasing shadows, fears long dead.
Across the void, they boldly soar,
With every flash, we seek for more.

A canvas painted, bold and wide,
Under its spell, we abide.
In the stillness, hearts awake,
Yearning for the paths we take.

Celestial rhythm, cosmic flow,
A journey where only dreamers go.
With every blink, the night declares,
The universe breathes in celestial flares.

The Hidden Depths of Night

In shadows deep, where secrets hide,
The moon reveals its silver tide.
Stars, like whispers, softly call,
In the silence, we can feel it all.

Mysteries dance on midnight's breath,
Echoes of life entwined with death.
Nothing spoken, everything shared,
In the dark, we find we're paired.

Veils of twilight cloak our fears,
Comfort found in silent tears.
In the dark, new worlds combine,
Unraveling with every sign.

Thoughts take flight in velvet skies,
Born of hope, they dare to rise.
Underneath, where dreams ignite,
There lies a beauty, pure and bright.

We wander through this mystic sea,
Lost in depths of mystery.
Together, hand in hand we roam,
In the night, we find our home.

Ethereal Moments in Time

A fleeting breath, a gentle sigh,
Time stands still, as dreams pass by.
Whispers linger, soft and light,
In the calm, we take to flight.

Each second drifts like clouds above,
Carried forth on wings of love.
Fleeting glimmers weave their way,
Turning dusk to break of day.

In the stillness, hearts will race,
Caught in a sweet, eternal place.
Softly spoken words transcend,
Moments shared will never end.

Every heartbeat, every tear,
Chronicles of those held dear.
Time, it dances, twirls and spins,
In the quiet, life begins.

Embrace the morn, let go the night,
In ethereal warmth, take flight.
For every instant, cherished rhyme,
Is a treasure in the hands of time.

Light Chasing the Darkness

Dawn breaks forth with golden rays,
Chasing shadows, igniting days.
Whispers of light sweep through the trees,
Awakening life with gentle ease.

Each beam a promise, bold and bright,
Piercing through the cloak of night.
Together, they dance on windowsills,
A symphony of warmth instills.

Waves of color brush the land,
In every corner, a guiding hand.
Light reveals what hides away,
In its glow, we find our way.

A journey starts with every rise,
Chasing shadows across the skies.
In its brilliance, hope takes flight,
Unraveling the depths of night.

Bright horizons come into view,
With every dawn, dreams are renewed.
In light's embrace, we find our spark,
Together facing the once-dark.

When Heaven Opens Up

The clouds part ways with grace,
A radiant light spills through.
Nature holds its breath in awe,
As colors dance anew.

The warmth of love descends,
Embracing all beneath.
Whispers of the gentle wind,
Carry dreams like wreaths.

Flowers bloom in joyful hues,
Painting fields with delight.
Every heart, it beats alive,
In the softness of the night.

Stars emerge, a twinkling show,
Guiding souls on their way.
Every wish sent to the sky,
With hope that it will stay.

In the stillness, time will pause,
As shadows fade away.
When heaven opens up so wide,
Love illuminates the day.

The Celestial Paradox

Stars laugh from their lofty perch,
While silence fills the space.
A swirling dance of light and dark,
In an eternal chase.

Each moment spun from ancient tales,
Woven in cosmic thread.
Mysteries lay in the void,
Where countless dreams are bred.

The night unveils its secrets bold,
Shooting stars take flight.
In the shadows, hope takes form,
Embracing the endless night.

Planets sing a timeless song,
With echoes from afar.
The universe, a paradox,
Where wishes meet a star.

In the depth of midnight's cloak,
The heart learns to believe.
In this grand celestial dance,
We find what we achieve.

Glistening Threads of Night

A tapestry of dreams is spun,
In the fabric of the dark.
Moonlight weaves its silver strands,
To ignite the hidden spark.

Whispers of the nightingale,
Echo through the trees.
As shadows play on velvet ground,
Captured by the breeze.

Each twinkling light a story told,
Of loves that crossed the sky.
With every heartbeat, hope takes flight,
A dance that won't say goodbye.

In silent hours, secrets breathe,
Veiled in the softest night.
The stars, they guide the wanderers,
To find their way to light.

A canvas painted bold and bright,
Awaits those brave enough.
In glistening threads of whispered dreams,
The night is pure, yet rough.

Horizons of Faint Aurora

The dawn breaks soft, a tender sigh,
Painting skies with hope.
Whispers weave through waking trees,
As light begins to cope.

Horizons blush in pastel strokes,
A dance of shades so rare.
Every heart feels alive once more,
Breathing in the morning air.

Gentle rays brush over hills,
Awakening the world.
Each petal opens, eager eyes,
In colors gently swirled.

The sun ascends, a golden crown,
Casting shadows long and wide.
With every beam, a promise glows,
In nature's gentle tide.

Horizons call, inviting all,
To rise and greet the day.
In faint auroras, life unveils,
The magic of our way.

The Secrets Weaved in Light

In shadows deep, the whispers sigh,
Threads of gold in twilight lie.
Stories fold in every ray,
Illuminating paths to stray.

Secrets dance on silver beams,
Carried softly through our dreams.
Veils of mystery gently part,
As light ignites the hidden heart.

Fleeting moments, time will keep,
In the light, our silence leap.
Fragments lost in evening's mist,
Echoes linger, can't resist.

Woven tapestries we find,
Messages from the divine.
In the glow, our fates entwine,
As shadows fade, our souls align.

Chasing beams in endless night,
Every shadow speaks of light.
Stories told in quiet grace,
In the dark, we find our place.

Moonlit Reflections

The silver orb hangs high above,
Casting dreams, a gentle love.
Rippling waters, still and clear,
Reflecting secrets, whispers near.

Beneath the stars, we drift and sway,
Time slows down, night turns to day.
In moonlit solace, hearts will mend,
Lost in thoughts that never end.

Shadows dance on ancient stone,
Echoes of the past now grown.
In the silence, we embrace,
The world transforms, a sacred space.

With whispered winds, the cool night air,
Holds the promise of a prayer.
Moonlit paths lead hearts anew,
In twilight worlds, our dreams break through.

Each glimmer holds a story told,
Of love unspoken, brave and bold.
As time drifts soft, we find our place,
In moonlit reflections, a warm embrace.

The Cloak of the Universe

Wrapped in starlit fabric, vast,
The cosmos sings of futures past.
Each star, a thread in endless dark,
Whispers of creation's spark.

Galaxies swirl in cosmic dance,
In every twinkle, a chance.
The veil of night, so deep, so wide,
Holds the mysteries that abide.

With each breath, the silence speaks,
The universe, in shadows, peaks.
Hidden wonders, waiting still,
To awaken the dreamer's will.

In every heartbeat, time unfurls,
The cloak of night, a treasure swirls.
Within its folds, we learn to see,
The truth that binds both you and me.

As stardust drifts through endless skies,
In every twinkle, a deep sigh.
The cloak remains, a silent guide,
In the universe, forever wide.

Beneath the Abyss of Beauty

In depths unknown, the colors blend,
A canvas where the shadows bend.
Whispers weave through silent night,
Beneath the abyss, reveals the light.

Fragile petals brush the air,
In beauty's depths, we find our share.
Every heartbeat, every sigh,
Life unfolds as stars drift by.

Lost in moments, soft and sweet,
The abyss cradles souls that meet.
In silence blooms a secret song,
Where broken pieces all belong.

A dance of dreams, a fleeting glance,
In twilight's grip, we take our chance.
Life's chaos finds its perfect place,
In beauty's arms, we find our grace.

Eternal depths will hold us tight,
As we explore the realms of light.
Beneath the abyss, love's beauty thrives,
In every heartbeat, each one alive.

Patterns of Twilight

In the hush of dusk's embrace,
Shadows dance upon the ground,
Colors blend in softest grace,
A whispered hush, a subtle sound.

Cloaked in violet, night takes flight,
Stars awaken, one by one,
Crickets sing, the moon shines bright,
The day is done, the night begun.

Waves of twilight brush the sky,
As dreams begin to intertwine,
Hearts unburden as they sigh,
In twilight's touch, the world aligns.

Fading light, a gentle kiss,
On mountains high, in valleys deep,
In twilight's glow, there lies pure bliss,
A moment held, forever steep.

So let the patterns softly weave,
A tapestry of night's delight,
In every heartbeat, we believe,
The magic found in patterns bright.

Illuminate the Infinite

In the shadows, secrets cling,
Whispers lost in endless night,
Stars above begin to sing,
Guiding souls with silver light.

With each flicker, stories bloom,
Of galaxies both near and far,
Mysteries in the vastness loom,
Each one a brilliant guiding star.

Journey forth through cosmic seas,
On waves of time, we float and sway,
Mapping dreams upon the breeze,
In starlit paths, we find our way.

Infinite tales of wonder spun,
Across the canvas of the sky,
We dance beneath the setting sun,
With open hearts, we reach and fly.

Illuminate what lies within,
The universe will softly glow,
In every heartbeat, life begins,
Together, we will learn and grow.

Wishing Upon Forgotten Stars

Silent night, a canvas bare,
The stars have dimmed, yet dreams arise,
In quiet corners, whispers flare,
We gather hope beneath dark skies.

Once bright wishes fade away,
Like echoes lost in realms of time,
Yet in our hearts, they still will stay,
A melody, a gentle rhyme.

With every flicker, a desire,
To touch the sky, to soar so high,
Reviving dreams, igniting fire,
We cast our hopes, like birds we fly.

The universe keeps silent watch,
On wishes penned in cosmic ink,
With every heartbeat, we will clutch,
The dreams that fade, the ones we think.

So gather 'round, as night unfolds,
And let us wish on stars once bright,
For every tale that time has told,
We find new light in lost starlight.

Cosmic Reflections

In the mirror of the night,
Galaxies swirl in cosmic dance,
Reflections gleam with borrowed light,
Inviting us to take a chance.

Every star, a story told,
Of ancient dreams and paths untrod,
In the silence, truths unfold,
Connecting us to all we are.

Whispers echo through the dark,
A symphony of shining grace,
In the void, we leave our mark,
With every heartbeat, we embrace.

The cosmos shimmers with delight,
Each spark a piece of who we are,
In endless trails of purest light,
We weave our fate among the stars.

So look within the infinite,
Reflect the beauty of your soul,
In cosmic realms, we are all it,
A part of love, a piece of whole.

Traces of Cosmic Tales

In whispers of starlight, dreams take flight,
Across the dark canvas, shimmer and bright.
Echoes of ancients dance in the skies,
Unveiling the secrets where the universe lies.

Galaxies twirl like leaves in the breeze,
Stories of ages carried with ease.
Time travelers drift on shimmering streams,
Weaving together the fabric of dreams.

Constellations glimmer, a map to the past,
Infinite wonders in shadows are cast.
Within the dark abyss, life takes its form,
A chorus of whispers, a cosmic storm.

Wonders of light, in silence they flow,
Guiding the lost through the celestial glow.
With every heartbeat, the cosmos inspires,
Fueling the passion that never tires.

So gaze at the heavens, let your heart soar,
In the fabric of time, there's always more.
Traces of tales that the stars have spun,
In the tapestry of life, we are all one.

The Astral Mosaic

Fragments of light, scattered and bright,
Creating a puzzle, an exquisite sight.
Each star a note in the grand cosmic song,
Together they weave what feels so wrong.

Nebulas blossom like flowers in space,
Colors collide in a delicate grace.
Patterns of time, forever they sway,
An astral mosaic, where dreams gently play.

Bound by the night, yet reaching for more,
The vastness invites us to explore.
Celestial rhythms in harmony spin,
Guiding our spirits, letting love in.

Shapes of existence in shadows reside,
Infinite wonders will forever abide.
Stories written in dust and in flame,
A celestial canvas that knows no name.

So follow the stardust, let it unfold,
A journey unique, as rare as gold.
In the cosmic embrace, we find our place,
A wondrous mosaic, the beauty of space.

Beyond the Horizon's Grasp

Where the sun kisses waves, dreams start to swell,
Beyond the horizon, where mysteries dwell.
The sky blushes softly, a canvas so wide,
Embracing the whispers of the ocean's tide.

Echoes of laughter in the salty breeze,
Time drifts like clouds, flowing with ease.
Footprints in sand, stories untold,
Waiting for wanderers, courageous and bold.

Each wave that crashes holds secrets anew,
The dance of the tides, a magical view.
Journey of souls as the dusk starts to fall,
Beyond the horizon, we surrender to all.

Colors ignite as the daylight departs,
Painting the heavens, igniting our hearts.
Stars awaken, one by one,
Glimmers of hope under the moon and sun.

So venture beyond where the light meets the sea,
In the embrace of night, let your spirit be free.
The horizon waits, a promise to keep,
In the depths of the night, the universe sleeps.

Night's Enigma Revealed

The moon whispers softly, secrets it knows,
Unveiling the mysteries where shadows impose.
In the silence of night, magic takes flight,
As dreams intertwine with the stars' gentle light.

Veils of illusion wrapped tenderly tight,
Guarding the wonders that slumber in night.
Through the stillness, a melody hums,
A symphony calling, as destiny comes.

Paths in the darkness, unseen yet profound,
Guiding the seekers who yearn to be found.
Each heartbeat resonates with the pulse of the dark,
Awakening visions, igniting a spark.

The cosmos conspires, revealing its art,
A tapestry woven with passion and heart.
In midnight's embrace, the stories ignite,
Unraveling wonders hidden from sight.

So embrace the enigma, let wisdom unfold,
In the cradle of night, mysteries are told.
With every breath taken, we rise and we feel,
The beauty of darkness, night's enigma revealed.

Dreams Beneath the Midnight Canopy

In shadows deep, the whispers weave,
A tapestry of dreams to believe.
Underneath the starlit glow,
Secrets of the night softly flow.

The moonlight paints the world in gold,
Stories of the night unfold.
A gentle breeze sings lullabies,
As visions dance in tranquil skies.

With every flicker, hopes arise,
The canvas vast, where magic lies.
In slumber's clutch, we drift away,
To realms where night meets break of day.

The stars above, a guiding hand,
Reflecting dreams we yearn to stand.
In midnight's warmth, we find our peace,
And let the fears of waking cease.

So linger on, dear night divine,
In your embrace, our souls align.
In dreams beneath this canopy,
We'll chase the night eternally.

Dance of the Glittering Night

Beneath the sky, the stars convene,
In symphonies of light, serene.
The whispers soft, they call our name,
In this luminous, enchanting game.

With every twinkle, hearts ignite,
In the dance of the glittering night.
Each flicker tells a story true,
Of wishes made, and dreams anew.

The moon spins slowly, a silver wheel,
A cosmic rhythm, we can feel.
In shadows cast, our spirits rise,
Bound by the magic of the skies.

The air is thick with dreams untold,
Where every heart can be so bold.
With outstretched arms, we find our wings,
And in the night, our laughter sings.

As dawn approaches, colors blend,
The dance of night begins to end.
Yet in our hearts, the spark remains,
A celebration of all our gains.

Starlit Reveries

In twilight hush, when shadows play,
The stars awaken the dreams of day.
A tapestry of light unfurls,
As night descends and whispers twirls.

With every breath, a vision wakes,
In starlit reveries, our soul breaks.
A universe within our reach,
Where silence speaks, and hearts can teach.

With constellations guiding our flight,
We navigate through the velvet night.
Each heartbeat synced with cosmic time,
In endless patterns, pure and sublime.

The moon, a guardian of our dreams,
Reflects the light of far-off beams.
Together in this cosmic sea,
We find the colors of you and me.

In every star, a wish is sown,
A promise made, no longer alone.
In starlit dreams, we learn to see,
The magic of eternity.

A Tangle of Twilight Threads

In twilight's grasp, where darkness spills,
A tangled weave of dreams and thrills.
Colors merge in fading light,
As the world prepares for night.

Threads of silver, strands of gold,
In whispers soft, their tales unfold.
Each thread a story, rich and bright,
Spun within the fabric of night.

With every turn, the shadows glow,
In this dance of ebb and flow.
A tapestry of hopes and fears,
Woven gently through the years.

In every corner, magic wakes,
With every heartbeat, the silence breaks.
A chorus filled with songs unsung,
In the web of dreams, we are young.

So let us weave, with skillful hands,
A world where wonder forever stands.
In twilight's arms, we find the reds,
A journey spun with twilight threads.

The Shimmering Horizon

The sun dips low, a golden ray,
Casting shadows as night holds sway,
Whispers of dusk in the gentle breeze,
Painting the sky with hues that tease.

Stars flicker on in the velvet dome,
Guiding the wanderers back to home,
Each twinkle a story, a light to share,
In the stillness, dreams float through the air.

The ocean sighs with a tranquil tune,
Reflecting the glow of the rising moon,
Waves dance softly on the sandy beach,
Where hearts are full and souls can reach.

In the pink and purple of twilight's song,
Hope awakens, where we belong,
Filled with wonder, as the night unfolds,
The shimmering horizon, a sight to behold.

Each moment captured, a fleeting spark,
Guiding us onward, towards the arc,
Together we stand, as day meets night,
Embracing the magic, and feeling light.

Echoes in the Astral Dark

In the vastness of the astral sea,
Echoes linger, wild and free,
Stars communicate with whispers low,
A cosmic dance in the dark's warm glow.

Nebulas swirl like dreams afloat,
Casting shadows, in silence they gloat,
Each planet hums a timeless song,
In the universe's heart, we all belong.

Constellations blink with ancient light,
Painting tales of love and plight,
Across the canvas of midnight blue,
A tapestry woven, forever true.

Galaxies spin in a graceful embrace,
Time and space, an enchanting chase,
Each moment echoes through the void,
Filling our hearts, never devoid.

In dreams, we wander the astral paths,
Discovering secrets, feeling the laughs,
With every starlit breath we take,
Whispers of infinity gently awake.

Luminous Horizons

A dawn breaks bright over hills so green,
Streaks of gold in the morning sheen,
Nature awakens with a vibrant pulse,
Each ray a promise, rich and convulse.

Mountains stand proud, kissed by light,
Guardians of dreams in the waking sight,
Silence speaks as whispers rise,
In luminous hues, the world replies.

Rivers glisten, a shimmering thread,
Carving paths, where many have tread,
With each flowing drop, stories unfold,
In reflections of time, tales are told.

As evening descends, a soft embrace,
Colors collide in a heavenly space,
The horizon glows, a canvas divine,
Painting our hopes, as stars align.

In twilight's hush, we find our dreams,
Illuminated by celestial beams,
Guided by light, forever we roam,
In luminous horizons, we find our home.

Woven Dreams of the Cosmos

In the quiet of night, dreams weave tight,
Stars twinkle softly, a mesmerizing sight,
Galaxies spin like stories untold,
Woven dreams of the cosmos unfold.

Each flicker calls to the heart's deep core,
Inviting us in to explore and soar,
Stardust dances in the midnight air,
As shadows lift, dissolving despair.

Planets align in a mystical trance,
A cosmic ballet, a timeless chance,
In every heartbeat, the universe sings,
Echoes of wonder as hope takes wing.

With every thought, we create our fate,
Crafting the fabric of what awaits,
Woven in harmony, love and light,
In the cosmos' embrace, we reunite.

So let us drift through this sacred space,
Finding our truth in the stars' embrace,
In dreams so vivid, we feel alive,
Woven dreams of the cosmos, we thrive.

The Nighttime Letter to the Universe

In shadows deep, I write to stars,
A hopeful whisper from afar.
Each twinkling light, a path untold,
In silent dreams, my heart unfolds.

Moonlight bathes my secret thoughts,
With every pulse, a wish is caught.
The universe hears my quiet plea,
In the still of night, I long to be free.

Galaxies spin with a tender grace,
Each letter etched in time and space.
I send my hopes on a silver thread,
To where the ancient cosmos spread.

Fingers trace the velvet sky,
As I reach out, I cannot lie.
With every star that meets my gaze,
I find the courage to embrace the haze.

So here I wait for signs divine,
In every moment, I will pine.
For in the dark, a love is spun,
A nighttime letter to everyone.

Threads of Cosmic Lull

In twilight's hush, a gentle thread,
Weaves through dreams, where spirits tread.
Stars hum softly, a lullaby's tune,
Dancing in rhythm with the pale moon.

Galaxies sigh, their stories take flight,
In the cradle of the deepening night.
Whispers of time in the cosmic flow,
Guide my heart where the wonders glow.

Nebulas bloom in colors so bright,
Casting shadows, painting the night.
In silence vast, I find my place,
Entwined with stars in their embrace.

Each twinkle a note in the cosmic song,
Lifting me up where I belong.
Threads of lull, a celestial weave,
In this embrace, I believe.

So close your eyes and drift away,
Let the cosmos dance and play.
I'll follow you where dreams run free,
In threads of cosmic jubilee.

Melodies Beneath a Black Canopy

Beneath the black, the night sings low,
Melodies soft, like a gentle flow.
Crickets chirp in a rhythmic spree,
Nature's symphony calls to me.

Stars alight in a velvet dome,
Each note a whisper, a wanderer's home.
In the hush of night, the world feels anew,
As echoes of dreams drift soft and true.

The moon casts shadows, soft and serene,
A silver glow on the earth's green sheen.
With every breath, the melodies wander,
In the stillness, my thoughts grow fonder.

Deep in the heart of the quiet sky,
Wisdom flows as the night winds sigh.
Under this canopy, dreams take flight,
Carried away by the pulse of the night.

So linger a while in this tranquil space,
Let time unravel in the soft embrace.
For within the night, the music flows,
Beneath the black, where the magic grows.

Lost in the Astral Sprawl

In the vast expanse, my spirit roams,
Lost in realms where no one knows.
Stars like diamonds in endless seas,
Whisper secrets with every breeze.

Planets spin in a silent dance,
Drawing my heart in a trance.
Through cosmic veins, I journey on,
In the light of the shifting dawn.

Galactic wonders pull me near,
As mysteries unfold, crystal clear.
In the astral sprawl, I find my peace,
A woven tapestry, a sweet release.

Beyond the bounds of time and space,
Each heartbeat an echo, a fleeting trace.
Among the stars, I learn to fly,
Embracing the vastness, I touch the sky.

So here I drift, in the cosmic sea,
With every breath, I set me free.
Lost in the starlit void, I dare,
To seek the endless, to dream and share.

When Stars Converse in Silence

When stars converse in silent night,
Whispers of dreams take delicate flight.
The cosmos breathes in gentle sighs,
As time drifts softly beneath dark skies.

In velvet depths, their secrets twine,
Each flicker holds a tale divine.
Celestial thoughts weave through the void,
In cosmic dance, we are all buoyed.

They tell of worlds just out of sight,
Of hopes and loves that feel so right.
A lullaby sung in twinkling beams,
Painting our hearts with starlit dreams.

Lost in the wonder of their glow,
In night's embrace, we come to know.
Each star a friend, a silent guide,
In the vast expanse where secrets hide.

So let us gaze and let us be,
Beneath the stars, wild and free.
For in their silence, stories blend,
And through the night, our souls ascend.

The Eventide Endures

The eventide endures, calm and still,
As shadows stretch with gentle will.
The sun dips low in a fiery glow,
Bathing the earth in a warm tableau.

Whispers of twilight softly blend,
In golden hues, the day we suspend.
A canvas of dreams in colors bold,
In every stroke, a memory told.

The stars awaken, one by one,
A tapestry crafted, dusk has begun.
Each twinkle a promise, a chance to see,
In the quiet of night, we can just be.

Eventide breathes, with a calming grace,
Embracing the night with a tender embrace.
In the hush of the dusk, all worries cease,
In every heartbeat, we find our peace.

As shadows dance to the moon's soft light,
We find respite in the tranquil night.
Thus, the eventide whispers its tune,
Cradling the earth beneath the moon.

Gaze Upon the Radiance

Gaze upon the radiance bright,
Where hopes emerge in morning light.
Each ray a promise, a brand new day,
Illuminating dreams along the way.

Golden beams cascade like streams,
Awakening souls, igniting dreams.
In every glimmer, joy is found,
Echoes of laughter that resound.

The world transforms in the dawn's embrace,
Renewed with purpose, grace fills space.
Nature rejoices, its colors sing,
In the warmth of the sun, we find our wings.

So let us gather, hearts open wide,
In the glow of hope, we shall abide.
Together we stand, hand in hand,
In the radiance, our dreams expand.

Gaze upon the beauty, let it ignite,
The spark within, our guiding light.
For in every sunrise, a story unfolds,
In the tapestry of life, our fate is told.

Out of the Shadows, Into the Light

Out of the shadows, we rise anew,
Into the light, where dreams come true.
With each step forward, we shed the past,
Embracing the dawn, our hearts beat fast.

The weight of fear begins to fade,
As courage blooms in the sunlight's glade.
In the brightness, we find our might,
Reclaiming our power, igniting the fight.

With open arms, we greet the day,
Casting aside doubts that led us astray.
For in the light, we find our way,
Building a future, come what may.

Our spirits dance in the warm embrace,
Of hope and love, a boundless space.
In unity, our voices soar,
Together, we stand, forevermore.

Out of the shadows, we take our flight,
With hearts ablaze, we chase the light.
For every ending leads to a start,
In the glow of dawn, we mend our heart.

Twilight's Enchanted Glow

The sky's a canvas, brushed in gold,
Whispers of secrets, softly told.
Shadows dance as light does fade,
In twilight's embrace, dreams cascade.

Stars awaken, one by one,
Bidding farewell to the setting sun.
Nature's silence, a gentle lull,
In this moment, the heart feels full.

Glowing hues in a mystic blend,
Promises of night that never end.
The world slows down, a calming sigh,
As twilight spreads across the sky.

A brush of lavender, the scent of peace,
Time slips away, allowing release.
The clouds adorned in hues so bright,
Holding magic in the fading light.

In this twilight, magic swirls,
As night unfurls, the wonder twirls.
Every heartbeat feels like a song,
In twilight's glow, we all belong.

The Lanterns of the Dark Sky

In the canvas of night, lanterns sway,
Guiding the lost along their way.
Shimmering softly, a warm embrace,
Lighting the paths that time can't erase.

Stars like candles, flickering bright,
Dancing in rhythm with the soft night.
Each flicker tells tales of old,
In whispers of wonder, secrets unfold.

Moonlight spills like silver grace,
Painting shadows, a soft trace.
The darkened skies wear a jeweled crown,
In the glow of lanterns, hope is found.

Breezes carry a tune so light,
As lanterns sway in the arms of night.
Echoes of laughter float on air,
In this embrace, we shed our care.

Together we walk, hearts intertwined,
Under the stars, all fears confined.
With every step, the past we mend,
In the glow of lanterns, love will send.

Celestial Murmurs

In the silence of night, whispers start,
Celestial murmurs, straight from the heart.
The cosmos hums its ancient tune,
Beneath the silver watch of the moon.

Galaxies twirl in a dance so grand,
Painting stories we don't understand.
Nebulas bloom in colors so rare,
Each twinkle a tale, floating in air.

Echoes of time in starlit flows,
Cascading dreams where the stardust glows.
In this vast space, we find a thread,
Binding our wishes to all that's said.

Through the heavens, old songs weave,
Melodies of life that we believe.
Under the night, souls take flight,
In celestial murmurs, hearts ignite.

With every twinkling, a spark we find,
In the tapestry of the cosmic mind.
Boundless whispers in twilight's shroud,
Echoing softly, forever loud.

Nocturnal Tapestry

Threaded in shadows, the night unfurls,
A tapestry woven with dreams and pearls.
Stars stitch memories, bright and bold,
In the fabric of night, stories are told.

The moon, a needle, weaves through the dark,
Sewing the whispers, each shimmering spark.
The world transforms under velvet skies,
With nocturnal threads that softly rise.

Creatures stir in the midnight hour,
In this tapestry, there's magic and power.
Gentle breezes carry tales of old,
In the warmth of night, we wait and behold.

Patterns of silence, embroidered so tight,
Each stitch a moment, glimmering bright.
Through the fabric, our spirits dance,
Unraveling secrets in the moon's glance.

A mosaic of dreams, vibrant and clear,
As the night whispers softly, come near.
In this nocturnal hug, we touch the divine,
With every thread, our hearts entwine.

When Darkness Holds a Dance

In shadows deep, the night awakes,
Whispers creep, and silence breaks.
The moonlight glows, a silver chance,
As stars above begin to dance.

A fleeting breath on autumn air,
With haunting tales of love and care.
Beneath the veil, the secrets sway,
As dreams collide, then fade away.

The heartbeats of the earth align,
In dark embrace, we intertwine.
Each flicker tells a story grand,
When darkness holds a guiding hand.

A world concealed in shadow's grace,
Where shadows flit and moments trace.
We find our truths in night's romance,
Amidst the stars, we take our stance.

And as the silence hums a song,
In nocturnal light, we all belong.
United in the dark's embrace,
When darkness holds a sacred space.

Enigmatic Horizons

Beyond the hills, where secrets lie,
Awaits the dawn, a painted sky.
Violet dreams in morning rays,
Unfolding truths in new displays.

Waves of colors, bold and bright,
The horizon calls, igniting light.
In every shade, the stories blend,
Enigmas formed, that never end.

The compass spins, the heart explores,
Across the worlds, unseen shores.
Each step reveals a wondrous sight,
A path unveiled, a soul's delight.

With every breath, the journey flows,
Through mystic realms where no one knows.
A dance of fate, forever chasing,
In search of dreams, there's no erasing.

Embrace the whispers of the day,
As shadows fade, and doubts give way.
The future glows with daring scenes,
In enigmatic skies, we find our means.

Twilight's Gentle Whisper

As daylight fades, a whisper calls,
In twilight's grasp, serenity falls.
Branches sway in a soft ballet,
Where dusk weaves dreams that drift away.

The stars emerge, a twinkling show,
Glimmers of hope in their gentle glow.
In twilight's arms, the world feels light,
A promise held by the coming night.

Colors merge in a tender embrace,
With every heartbeat, we find our place.
The softest breeze, a tender sigh,
In whispered tones, we learn to fly.

Moments linger, then fade like dust,
In twilight's realm, we find our trust.
With hearts aglow and spirits high,
We chase the dreams that fill the sky.

So come and dance where shadows play,
In twilight's warmth, we'll find our way.
The night awaits with secrets deep,
As twilight's whispers cradle sleep.

Gazing into Infinity

In starlit skies, our hopes take flight,
Gazing deep into the night.
Every spark, a tale untold,
Fractals in the dark unfold.

Like waves that crash on shores unknown,
We drift through realms where dreams are sown.
In cosmic dance, we lose our fears,
Embracing time that spans through years.

Each heartbeat pulses, steady, strong,
In the vastness, we all belong.
Connections formed across the dreams,
In unity, we find our themes.

A journey endless, yet so near,
In infinity, we feel no fear.
The universe whispers secrets sweet,
Inviting us to feel complete.

So here we stand, hand in hand,
With visions bright, we understand.
In endless night, we softly sigh,
Gazing into infinity, we fly.

.

Celestial Dreams Unfurled

In the still of night, stars gleam bright,
A tapestry woven in ethereal light.
Each twinkle whispers secrets untold,
As dreams take flight, brave and bold.

Comets dance across the moon's face,
While shadows drift in an endless embrace.
Galaxies spin in a waltz of grace,
In the realm of stars, we find our place.

A cosmic canvas, hues intertwined,
Nature's rhythm, perfectly aligned.
We close our eyes, let the magic unfold,
In celestial dreams, our hearts behold.

The silence sings a lullaby sweet,
In the cradle of night, our hearts meet.
With every breath, we reach for the skies,
Finding solace where the infinite lies.

So let us drift through this endless sea,
Guided by starlight, forever free.
For in the cosmos, we become one,
In the dance of time, where dreams are spun.

Whispers of the Night Sky

Under velvet skies, the night unfolds,
With starry whispers, mysteries told.
Each fluttering breeze carries secrets away,
In the embrace of night, we wish to stay.

Moonlight spills softly, a silver stream,
Cradling our hopes, fueling our dreams.
As shadows merge in the hush of dusk,
We find comfort in the night's soft husk.

The constellations shimmer, stories in flight,
Each glowing orb shines through the night.
In this quiet space, we find our dreams,
Along the edges of moonlit beams.

Time stands still as we gaze above,
The sky a canvas painted with love.
In the heart of the night, we lose our fears,
Finding solace within the starlit tears.

So let us wander where the whispers play,
In the serene embrace of the galaxy's sway.
For here in the dark, hope comes alive,
In the whispers of night, we truly thrive.

Luminous Dreams Unfurled

Awash in gleaming beams of light,
Dreams begin to dance in the night.
Each thought a spark, a radiant flow,
In the luminous glow, we learn to grow.

Nights painted bright with colors untamed,
All souls united, no one is shamed.
Under a sky that embraces our plight,
A tapestry woven with dreams shining bright.

The echo of wishes calls out in the dark,
Lighting the path with hope's gentle spark.
With every heartbeat, passion ignites,
In luminous dreams, we find our flights.

Letting go of fears, we reach for the stars,
In the grand expanse, we heal our scars.
Every glow a symbol of what could be,
In luminous shadows, we seek to be free.

So come, take my hand, let us explore,
Through luminous dreams, forevermore.
In the embrace of light, we find our song,
Together we'll dance, where we belong.

Celestial Tapestry

Woven threads of silver and gold,
Stories of the universe patiently told.
In the fabric of night, starlight does weave,
A celestial tapestry we dare to believe.

Each stitch a moment, a wish, a prayer,
A reminder that magic is everywhere.
The moon spins tales of love and loss,
In the heart of the night, we bear our cross.

Nebulae drifting on the edge of time,
Dancing in rhythms, a cosmic rhyme.
Planets in orbit, secrets they keep,
In this grand quilt, our souls dive deep.

Whispers of time in the dark expanse,
The galaxy's heartbeat invites us to dance.
In the celestial blend of dusk and dawn,
We find our place, where we belong.

As we gaze into the vast unknown,
In the weave of existence, we find our own.
So let us cherish each luminous thread,
In the celestial tapestry, our dreams are spread.

A Tapestry of Infinite Night

Beneath the starry shroud so deep,
Colors weave in silence, sleep.
Threads of dreams and shadows blend,
A canvas vast that has no end.

Whispers echo in the dark,
Guiding souls to leave their mark.
Each twinkle holds a story told,
In the night, both young and old.

The moon, a sentinel of grace,
Bathes the world in soft embrace.
A lighthouse through the endless sea,
Of time, of space, eternity.

In this realm where secrets hide,
Wonders bloom, and fears subside.
A tapestry of love and light,
Enduring through the endless night.

Stars are born from ancient dreams,
In the dark, a beauty gleams.
Each fold a wish, a silent plea,
A tapestry, forever free.

Secrets of the Midnight Veil

The night unveils its hidden charms,
A gentle hush, a world in arms.
Moonlit paths of whispered wind,
Where secrets of the shadows begin.

Gentle echoes ride the breeze,
Unraveling truths among the trees.
Each rustle holds a cryptic sign,
In the veil, the stars align.

Beneath the cloak of midnight's grace,
Lies a dance, a cosmic chase.
Stars entwined with fate's embrace,
In soft shadows, we find our place.

What stories wait in silent stones?
Of ancient dreams and whispered tones?
In the dark, we find our way,
A map of night, forever stay.

Secrets twinkle with every sigh,
As the moon watches from on high.
In the mystery of the calm,
Lies the world's most soothing balm.

Timeless Whispers in the Void

In the vastness where moments wane,
Whispers echo, soft as rain.
Timeless echoes of what has been,
In the void, where dreams begin.

Galaxies spin in endless dance,
Each twinkling light a fleeting glance.
Crickets sing their nightly song,
In the stillness, we belong.

Infinite realms await our call,
Hidden treasures behind the fall.
With each breath, we weave the thread,
Of stories written, hearts we'll spread.

Every sigh is a timeless plea,
Carried forth through history.
As the cosmic winds begin to stir,
The void whispers, a gentle purr.

Hold the silence, feel it near,
In the emptiness, love is clear.
Whispers rise and softly fade,
In the void, all dreams are made.

Mosaic of Cosmic Reflections

Fragments of stars, a grand display,
Each piece a wish, lost in sway.
A tapestry of cosmic lore,
Reflects the dreams we long for more.

Every planet spins a song,
In this dance, we all belong.
Celestial rhythms pulse and glide,
In the night where hopes reside.

Colors merge in starlit beams,
Painting life from countless dreams.
The universe, a canvas bright,
Mosaic formed of love and light.

Time unfolds in spirals high,
As comets dart across the sky.
Each heartbeat syncs with cosmic flow,
In the still, celestial glow.

In this dance of dusk and dawn,
We find the spark that's never gone.
A mosaic that will ever bloom,
In the night, dispelling gloom.

Beneath the Cosmic Cloak

Stars whisper secrets to the night,
Nebulas dancing in soft twilight.
Galaxies twirl in a cosmic spin,
While dreams of wanderers begin.

Planets spin, draped in stardust fine,
Gravity pulls in a celestial line.
Comets trail tales through endless skies,
Beneath the cosmic cloak, the universe lies.

Silent orbs in a vast expanse,
Invite the quiet for a gentle dance.
Fractals of light in a boundless sea,
Calling the heart to set it free.

Whispers of time in the void they roam,
Charting the course of the unknown home.
In shadows deep and galaxies bright,
Under the cloak, all feels just right.

So linger we must where the stardust flows,
In the heart of the night, where wonder grows.
A tapestry woven through cosmic threads,
Beneath the cloak, where adventure spreads.

Flickering Echoes of Light

In the stillness, shadows dance,
Flickering flames in a trance.
Whispers echo through the night,
Sketching tales in shards of light.

Memories flicker like stars on high,
Remnants of laughter, a fleeting sigh.
A heartbeat pulses in the dark,
As echoes find their sacred spark.

Fragments of joy and shades of pain,
Twist through moments like falling rain.
Each sparkle tells a story untold,
Of love, of loss, in hues of gold.

In the silence, we gather near,
Chasing the flickers, holding dear.
For in the echoes, we find our place,
Illuminated by time's gentle grace.

So let us wander through paths unknown,
Finding light in the seeds we've sown.
Flickering echoes shall guide our way,
As night gives birth to another day.

Mystique of the Ether

Veils of mist cloak the twilight air,
Whispers of secrets, shadows rare.
In the ether, dreams arise,
Dancing softly beneath the skies.

A tapestry woven of whispers and sighs,
Starlit pathways, where silence lies.
Mysteries pulse in the cosmic stream,
Boundless and bright, a lucid dream.

Echoes of time spin like dust in light,
Guiding the way through the velvet night.
In every breath, a story unfurls,
Infinite wonders of unseen worlds.

Through the ether, a symphony plays,
Notes carried soft in a timeless haze.
With each flicker of night's gentle breath,
We delve deeper, in wonder bequeath.

So let us wander where shadows sigh,
Under the expanse of the endless sky.
In the mystique of ether's embrace,
We find our truth in the moon's soft grace.

Constellation's Breath

In the deep where the silence sings,
Constellations whisper of hidden things.
Each star a story, each light a thread,
Woven in tales where lovers tread.

Galactic blooms in a velvet sea,
Map the dreams of you and me.
In the night sky, our hearts combine,
Under the gaze of the divine.

Flickers of hope in the cosmic dance,
Invite the brave to take a chance.
Wander souls through the stellar gate,
Writing our fate before it's too late.

With every breath, the cosmos sighs,
A gentle touch where the universe lies.
In the embrace of the night's caress,
We discover love's eternalness.

So linger beneath the radiant light,
Hold tightly to dreams that burn bright.
In the constellation's breath, we find,
A pathway for the heart and mind.

The Night's Illuminated Canvas

Stars dance on a velvet sky,
Whispering tales of dreams gone by.
Moonlight spills like silver wine,
Painting the world in soft divine.

Clouds drift like thoughts in the breeze,
Carving shadows among the trees.
Each glimmer holds a story bright,
A canvas crafted by the night.

Gentle winds play a soft tune,
Filling hearts under the moon.
Nature's brush paints fierce and free,
A masterpiece for all to see.

Time suspends in tranquil glow,
As constellations ebb and flow.
Beneath the stars, we dream anew,
In the canvas bright, me and you.

Life's secrets hidden in each shade,
In stillness, the moments cascade.
With every twinkle, hope ignites,
In the night's illuminated sights.

Radiant Shadows

In twilight's hush, shadows grow,
Secrets whispered, soft and low.
Moonbeams touch the silent ground,
In radiant beauty, lost yet found.

Darkness cradles truth untold,
In shadows cast, dreams unfold.
The night's embrace, gentle and wide,
Guides the hearts that wish to bide.

Flickers of light weave through the dark,
Each moment held, a hidden spark.
In every shadow, a story waits,
A dance of chance, our fates create.

Time lingers in the fading light,
Crafting echoes of day and night.
A radiant glow, electric thrill,
In quiet moments, love we fill.

Underneath the starry sheet,
Life unfolds in rhythmic beat.
In the stillness, magic flows,
In radiant shadows, beauty grows.

Secrets in the Starlight

Amidst the night, whispers gleam,
Secrets lie in the silver beam.
Every twinkle hides a tale,
In starlight's grip, hopes set sail.

Cosmic currents speak so clear,
In silence, our wishes appear.
Under vast and endless skies,
Dreams awaken, gently rise.

Constellations weave our fate,
In celestial patterns, we wait.
The dance of light, a brief parlay,
Guides our hearts along the way.

In shadows cast by glittering bright,
We find our truths in the deep night.
Each secret forged in cosmic fire,
Ignites the soul's most fervent desire.

Stars align with a knowing smile,
Chasing darkness for a while.
Underneath the heavens' sight,
We cherish secrets in the starlight.

Midnight's Glimmering Cloak

Midnight drapes the world in dark,
A glimmering cloak with a touch of spark.
Whispers lie where shadows fall,
In the night's embrace, we heed the call.

A tapestry of dreams unfolds,
In silver threads, the magic holds.
With every gust, the stories wake,
Underneath this midnight make.

The stars align in whispered song,
Guiding wayfarers to where they belong.
Through hidden paths, under the moon,
Lies the promise of a gentle tune.

Each heartbeat echoes in silence vast,
Moments captured, shadows cast.
In the soft glow, we find our way,
Through midnight's charm, come what may.

Embrace the night with fervent grace,
For in its cloak, we find our place.
With open hearts and spirits bright,
We weave our dreams in the endless night.

www.ingramcontent.com/pod-product-compliance
Ingram Content Group UK Ltd.
Pitfield, Milton Keynes, MK11 3LW, UK
UKHW031955131224
452403UK00010B/549